THE SOFT PATH

AKRON SERIES IN POETRY

AKRON SERIES IN POETRY
Mary Biddinger, Editor

Joshua Harmon, *The Soft Path*
Oliver de la Paz, *The Boy in the Labyrinth*
Krystal Languell, *Quite Apart*
Brittany Cavallaro, *Unhistorical*
Tyler Mills, *Hawk Parable*
Caryl Pagel, *Twice Told*
Emily Rosko, *Weather Inventions*
Emilia Phillips, *Empty Clip*
Anne Barngrover, *Brazen Creature*
Matthew Guenette, *Vasectomania*
Sandra Simonds, *Further Problems with Pleasure*
Leslie Harrison, *The Book of Endings*
Emilia Phillips, *Groundspeed*
Philip Metres, *Pictures at an Exhibition: A Petersburg Album*
Jennifer Moore, *The Veronica Maneuver*
Brittany Cavallaro, *Girl-King*
Oliver de la Paz, *Post Subject: A Fable*
John Repp, *Fat Jersey Blues*
Emilia Phillips, *Signaletics*
Seth Abramson, *Thievery*
Steve Kistulentz, *Little Black Daydream*
Jason Bredle, *Carnival*
Emily Rosko, *Prop Rockery*
Alison Pelegrin, *Hurricane Party*
Matthew Guenette, *American Busboy*
Joshua Harmon, *Le Spleen de Poughkeepsie*

Titles published since 2011.
For a complete listing of titles published in the series,
go to www.uakron.edu/uapress/poetry.

THE SOFT PATH

JOSHUA HARMON

The University of Akron Press
Akron, Ohio

ISBN: 978-1-629221-82-3 (paper)
ISBN: 978-1-629221-83-0 (ePDF)
ISBN: 978-1-629221-84-7 (ePub)

A catalog record for this title is available from the Library of Congress.

∞The paper used in this publication meets the minimum requirements of ANSI/NISO z39.48–1992 (Permanence of Paper).

Cover image: *Transmission towers in fog*. Photograph by Neven Krcmarek on Unsplash. Cover design by Amy Freels.

The Soft Path was designed and typeset in Jenson, with Avenir Next display, by Amy Freels and printed on sixty-pound natural and bound by Bookmasters of Ashland, Ohio.

Affordable Learning Initiative
THE UNIVERSITY OF AKRON

Produced in conjunction with the University of Akron Affordable Learning Initiative. More information is available at www.uakron.edu/affordablelearning/

To S., and to M.,
and to I.F.

CONTENTS

our lives

are now

Someplace else

. . .

. . .

—Ed Roberson,
Atmosphere Conditions

"The choice between the soft and hard paths is urgent. Though each path is only illustrative and embraces an infinite spectrum of variations on a theme, there is a deep structural and conceptual dichotomy between them. Soft and hard *technologies* are not *technically* incompatible: in principle, nuclear power stations and solar collectors can coexist. But soft and hard *paths* are *culturally* incompatible: each path entails a certain evolution of social values and perceptions that makes the other kind of world harder to imagine. . . . And they are *logistically* competitive: every dollar, every bit of sweat and technical talent, every barrel of irreplaceable oil, every year that we devote to the very demanding high technologies is a resource that we cannot use to pursue the elements of a soft path urgently enough to make them work together properly."

—Amory B. Lovins, prepared testimony to the United States Senate, December 9, 1976

HOLYOKE RANGE

Bluish ice
sharded

on river
-bank: blunt

force instrument
-als of ice jam

improv sent down
-stream: crystal

-line slabs milled
to CNC

specs: a drift
adrift, frac-

tured floe
flowing past

broken window
-ed red brick

facts toward
falls: copies

fabricating copies
of themselves

amid the small-mol-
ecule current:

monotonic
harmonics, glis-

sandi of S4
frazil ice

water-glazed
into, against

itself like a self
-ie's intervent-

ions, sustain
-ing functions:

increased margins
of midwinter's

boom-and
-bust temps: bent

tone river
-bend: minor

shifts and settle
-ments: what's

as obscure
as day: era

of simulcast
endless disast-

ers compound
-ing interest

on lasting
zero weather:

CASCADING FAILURES

Snow against wind
-shield and snow, wind

-smoothed and -compressed
from undiminishing

source: snow's thirty-two
-feet-per-second-squared
low-tech sabotage

fixes me, hill
-middled amid head
-lit, highbeamed glitter:

Franchise the birches,
purchase the field's
receivables:
through windows
and winter's inter-

cessions, a pan
-orama unrushed
at 73 mph, 45.8 mpg,
190 deg. F.: but

snow's only a series
of 1x1 pixel GIFs

tracking me, Quinnehtukqut
to Quaboag, horizontal
-ly slivered, inelegantly torn
to pieces: a molecule:

In the passing lane
car lights catch
the modes of dust
and ash

and the motes of self
-ishness: the single pass
-enger's E-ZPass

odes of tires and potholed
luck: roads
-ide ghosts and chevrons
shining red

where guardrails and
guardedness end
the redund-

ancies in place
for potential failures
and other under
-corrections:

Cumulonimbus
aura, split to
the interior high

-lands: weak sunlight
scans trees' bar
codes: a discount

-ed grief we share
for the space of six
weeks, as if speech gives

us some other or
-nament: whatever
silence suggests,

an echo's use
-less aftermath: R-
value in two

feet of snowpack,
cloudfrazzle
on half a hill:

Brittle maples displaced
me, fenced-off
fragment of

field defaced:
the oscillations of the un-
housed self snowroaded,

winterfered with: an
irruption of red
-polls, the resonant peaks

of the Berkshires and band
-width's speaking
terms with terrain's int-

entions, pasture dis-
entitled by imperfectly
grounded wires: and a diesel

engine running a 20%
bio-blend grinds down
-ed trees to chips:

Amid a fine mist
of sawdust
carried by a faint
northeasterly:
we've got at least
a quarter
of this tree on
the ground already:
homespun un-
utterings, so much
labor undone
by a buy
-er's market:
the latest
comer goes:

A hundred twenty-one
miles cannot be made
to vanish: this never
-ender others me:
easy to forget
I am merely a one
-time programmable: low
reservoir, lower sun,
zero vim: but the heart
still blusters its watt
and a half, its boot-code
logic unarguable:

The front
-ier infrastructure in
-stalled ahead:
toll bar
-rier's license
plate capture be
-neath infinite
-ly irreproducible
clouds, utter brevity
of transit: two
-inch screen, dead head
-phones, crosstalk sky,
lah-de-dah weather
flash, lone
contrail's fuzz
-line fraying
horizonward:

Monosyllabic
wind's analog
dialogue at last
its last self

Meaning's made
unbecoming
by the fundamentals
unmaking one's history, like
26,000+ psi
direct-injected
becomes an every
-day spin over the hills
and away: and a for
-gotten password
atomizes Taconic
reluctance while
time's compression
goes on resonating along
remote sidings: but on
sky-strafed wave heights
remote is relative
to no kin's orphan
-ed technologies:

A cloud form
-ation, deform

-ed by an Air
-bus 380

tracking west-northwest
past my impermanent

sincerity: radio
silence: a pressure

wave: a snowlapse
under synthetic

cirrus, divested
of its nuance

by mid-morning
visions: the sun's

on the other side:
the barometric

altimeter reads
679′

and atop Tinker
Hill wind through oak

limbs is only
another engine:

Autumnalography's three
-lobed spike against cloud
-ragged sky: listening
stations in geotagged
woods, a system to bring
wires down:
the 600 kW day permits
us shadow-flicker
at a thousand-foot set
-back: echo edges:

Woods

-moke
in the air

vents

Anthemic pines this
morning frisk micro-
waved skies for what
completes the sent
-ence three F-15s curl
-ing ahead of their north
-wind roar assert: but,
below, a bush-flagged
bag snaps, and oak
leaves underfoot
overlay the root
-ed re-route
deep in the deep
-est woods avail
-able: the pass
-word-protected path
to the most technical
terrain serves a heavy
need: my equity
in this traprock
ridge and its out
-sourced austerity:

A satellite directs a semi
through eroded folds and up
-lifts beveled by years the pines
can't mark, the fine
-st-grained matrix of gravel
roads and numbered routes,
braidplains, valley choker
moraines: the primitive
premise of the interstate shield
-ing pictorial tributaries
from targeting plans and more
difficult questions, or the pro
-liferation of roadside asters
engineered for compliance
when the semi Jake-brakes
the downgrade, descending
the abstractions to some
plausible Housatonic:

A station's vast
-ly under
-stated devast
-ation: light

-headed fueling,
half-life of flame
kindling a median
strip in a median

state: post-cap
-italist worth
-lessness wavers
its signals:

Hilltown recon on
a humid mid-
summer forenoon:
flora partition
of thimbleweed, tick
-clover, purple vetch, ditch
lilies along a 12%
gravel grade: road edge
monocrop chokepoint:
everything doubled
and deprecated,
an abandonware town
indexed to no search
engine: landscape version
8.3: and then
a smudged swipescreen loops
bright-band backscatter,
thunderheads thrum
over a chipseal
lane banked with granite
riprap for runoff:

A new five-acre
solar ar-
ray's in ar-
rears after
seven cloudy days

This morning's
cirrostratus,
windshorn, contrail
-torn, through
bug-begrimed
safety glass:
halftone
hillsides own
only one
color: tam-
arack rack:

Sought the dryslot
in the doppler, the top
-ography in digitized
radio pulses real-timed
and memorialized
under widest wide
-screen sky: semantic
sky, insomniac sky, sani-
tized sky with absent
aether, hole-punched
cumulus above tranced trees,
hi-def hymn of honor
-ary moon as air
chimed my hills: droners
overheard: loose ends:

The soft path,
the signal path's
purity: branching
ahead of clouddata
and the freest
enterprises: the
404 error of sky
-line at twilight,
line of headlights,
what a corrective less
-ening sees: ghost
times to run
down: the bland
-ishments:

HORIZONTAL DROPOUTS

—and I, in between, unreachable,
elsewhere, otherwise: minor coordinate
dislocated on two-lane corridor,
pinned with eighteen-foot
accuracy to a curve in the spine
of hills the asphalt obeys
unwillingly in thinning afterdawn,
head headed already home
as the body leaves it: it's good
to see you: consider it
an opportunity: I'll do this
as long as they'll let me, though
I don't own the decision
and don't know who does: but only
five miles later, the sun
disappears, replaced by striations
of a need that stretches horizon
to horizon, bottom-line news
ticker scrolling past
off-ramp and on-ramp, radials
shredded on rolled-in rumble
strip, persistent stains where animals
bled, front-end dents on steel
W-beam guardrail,
injection-molded crumbs caught
in non-native grasses: so many
daily impressions, disabled
expressions: the eros of one
maple branch rubbing another in
a resolute northwest wind:

so

many connections
I can't keep, no

longer follow: everything
that seemed vital before I came
to terms with manifold
insignificances, forgot a sense
of how the pasture exists
for the bobolink: these
grains, those: a patent coded
in each seed atop the wind
-ruffled stalks: a feed: a flutter: a few
syllables stacked against compiled
days, bitmapped grid
of middlingest continuance:

                                        past
the border of the rest
area, behind fourteen canopied fuel
pumps, a cell-phone tower pretends
it is a tree, a second-growth signal
boost to five bars under the dying surface
low flowing east: but hills with holes render
the radar redundant, virga rain
as invisible as thinking
some underlit midday cloudslash
above Minnechoag proposes
a logical metaphor for
divinity's presence or
absence: the record
only extends the distance to return
to later, mid-pause, after the millionth
-of-a-second segments, untouched
and retouched, dithered,
cohere:

          I grew up never wanting
more than what I wanted

so intensely it became unreal, the way
printer's gradations of pale
and paler green register
topographies in the blankest
spaces, as blank as driving
the same parkway sixteen times
a month to mark goldenrod's nod
beneath breeze, goldfinch-seeded
thistles and milkweed grown
tall in a sumacked powerline
scar, chlorophyll fade to first frost
-blackened ends, two-wheeled plastic
garbage bins rolled aside a gravel
turnoff and emptied there, left
upended until the wind rearranges
the scene or some sedan returns to
a garage, until whatever slow
unplanned progress fails,
until an orange snow
fence blocks this data
field and black ice sets
after afternoon's
sun-struck edges:
                                        but what is
want if not a refusal
of our own erasures: as blank
as my frugal imagination
could muster: blank as the zeroes
the instruments logged:
blank as a desire
informed by someone else's
desire:
                pictorial notes:

veined and sunglitzy
granite, histories of headwinds
in snarls of stunted oaks, the scope
of reconnaissance like an inbred
self-obsession, and these fringe
phenomena appear and recede:
another pass-through entity,
a variable foreground
on a twisting grade where a driver's
engagement with road and terrain
reduces the accident rate, reduces
the unaccidental ratio
of person to auto:

1:1:

consider the optics:
it's all abstraction, a printout of exposure
and uncompensated expense,
a state return declaring
unlikely losses: so many
freeze/thaw cycles:
magnoscopic blues, blue
-and-red lightbar strobing half
a mile of highway's high
meadow and pines stressed rust
by exhaust: a spinout: traffic
squeezes left, but to the right streams
have eroded ravines through
the escarpment: basalt
talus on the steepest trails,
ground clutter fucking
the RF signal, oxidized
pylon 24.4 feet
south of three eight-inch paper

birches, granular rock with scattered feldspar
megacrysts in a cut on I-90, faded
tag on a concrete truss holding up
a sixty-year-old overpass needing
$1.8 million in repairs,
fingertip script in soot
on a trailer door:
a 2-D screenshot of a curved
world it seems less and less
possible to recognize: to inhabit:
what's terminally daybroken:
the person I was, the place
I left only yesterday
carrying another cardboard box
packed with years of paper: but lost
my receipt: I sought transparency,
but the graphical interface
shields the user from the system
and its complexities, the decisions
involving no less than a sense of risk's
futures, and no more: and the exploit
is limited to obsolete devices:
northern hardwoods regenerated
to large-pole stage on hills
once cleared for hayfields:
                                        hazard lights
hazard what a dozen doves
roosting on high-tension
tower ignore, but momentum
slows in accordance with
the figures of conceptual sleet
on Berkshire topos: with the fundamentals
of notation, the buffer of brake

lights: bare branches, broken, rifle
exurban lawns beyond the right
-of-way and its barbed fence
overgrown, woven with wasted
nightshade, bittersweet gone brown,
dried ragweed racemes: but no pause
lasts, nothing waits to await
nothing, and the theory at work
is a glareproof, shatterproof
display's doppler loop on
auto-refresh, whether weather will gloss
asphalt or allow an evening
return:
            the second-cheapest station's diesel
at $4.04/gal., and the daily debt
collection calls for
the ghost of a renter accumulate
unanswered in the phone's minimal
memory: an oil-truck delivery
of dyed #2: a prescription
for someone else's ailment
ready for pickup:
it won't be: my backward
desire to remain
in an eastern woodslope's
morning shade, a watertower's
good graces, the company
of rerun overtones, so I switch
off the ringer:
                        I can no longer
reduce the unknown at the edges
of my own dissipations: white pine
and white roadstripe, white

cross staked at the gap in the barrier
where a body left
the lane and laid itself down
four years ago, dynamited
bedrock still scored with the lines
of its own breakings, drained swamp
of mud-black wrack and stumps
below terraformed bluff a Case 580
Super M scrapes, shapes: a growth
industry in Japanese maples mulched
on a Massachusetts front lawn
greened with glyphosate, diazinon,
MCPP, isazophos, droplets
of potable water from in-ground
sprinklers beaded on each blade
-cut blade of fescue until the sun
evaporates them: a panoramic
austerity as, commuting, we commute
energy to air and air
returns it to us: squall lines
with stratiform rain: bow echo
scouring the valley before
breakup: or an EF3
that deforests thirty-nine miles
of suburbanized mixed
hardwood ridges, shifts sillplate
from foundation and scatters
shingles and sheathing, topples
chimneys, sunders steeples, splinters
us, then lifts itself and departs:
we are willing
nothing less:
                    the only stated

obligation is to repair or replace
the defective product:
                                    I checked
my phone to find
out where I was:
                              what endures
a fragment
-ed reading of fragments, a part
-ial attention to a flooded streambank
seen only at 70+ mph
beside which rises, incomplete
after two years, a galvanized
high-mast light pole
without lights: strawgrass
wavers in waters
that course somewhere to somewhere
else via a corrugated alloy
culvert, a plot of discharge
versus time as a ripple moves
downstream: the ambient atmosphere
limits the turbo's power,
but the engine burns lean
on the air/fuel mix and this
is my exit:
                    B1: 4: 10: 7:
                                    I can no longer
reside in the fictions overlaying
an event already wrinkled
by scrutiny, blunted with
recordings ripped into flash
memory at 320 kbps:
the boredom of a fixed
location, a hitch

in the throat from saying too much
or too little, a landscape observed
in portrait orientation, a rendering
engine, a post-encryption
treeline, a compression
algorithm so the file fits:
                                                the sound
I heard and the sound I dreamed
I heard:
                wind through the smallest
apertures, endlessly consoling treble chant
of crickets, bee-bothered purple asters
softening sand-striped backroads
these diminishing afternoons before work
crews clearcut twenty-yard swathes
verging the interstate: in another year or two
years, blackberry and burdock thicket
will grow back among unground
stumps and limbs left to weather
on the hillside, but now: how
to memorize scrub brush and saplings
fed into a chipper's hydraulic hopper,
heaps of trees:
                              the swift diminishment
of daylight this month indexes the earth's
elliptical orbit, so the pleasures
of a route's routine remain the only
ones one's allowed oneself
to feel, as grapevines'
persistent perfume yields
to the litter of discarded, defaulted
maple leaves cars scatter
moving past rapid

exteriors: it looked through
the fogged windshield like the sunset
contained its own motion
and motioned our containments:
Sevenmile River, Fivemile River,
deoxygenated lesser
ponds, Sucker
Brook, Winimusset Brook,
several seeps and intermittent
rills, Ware River: the spaciousness
of the narrowest valleys,
the gestures I never used,
memory's inevitabilities,
an exhausted self unable to stay
put but longing for this moment
to suspend itself, this economy-size
sky to remain on infinite repeat:
and nothing to do but keep driving
at the same argument I already
lost: and no longer believe:
downshift to third to crest
the rise, the ride
hesitates:
                    and the sound approaches
and exceeds 0 dB, drops out
from 0:27 to 0:32, some
hard-drive glitch,
overwritten bits:
                              got stuck
behind a farm-plate truck
well below the limit along tireworn double
yellow: aged asphalt nearly invisible
under sand and runoff, nothing but surface

and verge, cattails and phragmites shedding
fluff in a shrub bog as violet hours
slump into the terms silence sets
and point-blank dusk dissolves
a day's scriptures: as you revise
you might consider: hawthorn
rooted to an eroding roadbank:
I wanted a phrase
to speak for an absence
of endings:
                    impossibly:
                                        the last
late daydowned light
only a shiny speck aloft, tracking
at Mach .85: solar reflections
on 7075-T6 aluminum
skin and the paired
vapor trails turbines
loose: but amid stripped
trees off 148 N nothing's left
to explain an innate
resistance to civilization's force
multipliers but cordwood stacked
in a driveway:
                        I once believed in
the linear relationship between
a starved fire's sideways smoke
and a severance contained inside
parentheses, between depleted chances
and a drive to the next town, but not
the town after that, or the one after
an inventory of what we might
exchange for these unfaithful orchards,

a planning board draft for an eighty-one-
acre parcel, a court-ordered survey
for a transcontinental cable line:
the application of M.G.L., Ch. 40B:
believed in the buyback
program for a crossroads sugarbush:
in the affidavit of frostproof
foreign chrysanthemums blooming cerise
and amaranth and titian under
the same dull skies as always: in
everything I abandoned
before a proper valuation:
                                        mixed-use
development and adaptive re-use,
legibility of spaces
to articulate the difference:
                                          the protest
group submitted
to the settled question:
                                      the existing
conditions and property
lines, the abutting houses,
wetland boundaries, the
conveyance, an open meeting
no one attended, and the lawyer
resigned from the board:
                                        two
radio towers south of Wine Road blink
above a hummocked pasture's long
grass shadows encircled by electrified
wire: dusk doubles the afternoon's
overcast, and slo-mo snows of yellow
birch and ash leaves

from the fenced-off government
property break up
the footage from the feed: water's
least resistant path downhill explains
the most recognizably human
element of this place, but not
the only human element: an heirloom,
a penalty, a little careless
music to ease one's passage, a routing
number for the automated
monthly direct deposit, bad
data as the signal drifts,
an impossible cadence,
another vapid interior
registering its say-so:
and the twenty-five-year
return comes in on an un-
repaired dam, the remains
of glacial retreat, a credit
check:
          nothing can be
restored, not even
a duplicate file:
                    and night
again: offset supermoon
disk slips above Pattaquattic,
clear of adblocked clouds
to legitimize this record: overhead's
only a seamless stitched sphere
of digitized stars: I can surrender
hours, too, years even, but what do
you call it when the progress
bar hangs up before the end and

refuses to finish: and what ever
finishes: not concrete feelings
of awe, not the occasion
to become a footprint:
                                        a footnote:
the class 8C
truck idling off the off-ramp,
amber running lights that seem
as real as the leftovers of self
-concern:
                  the rain did this, not
me:
        and a null space after the inevitable
encounter, what happens every
autumn: a present-tense burial,
a microchasm of months
I never think will arrive
until they arrive, a window
open overnight to admit
cold air:
                the road bottoming
one of the loneliest valleys I know
changes surface and name three times
as it crosses town lines, its last mile
engineered at a steady grade
to escape those steep slopes,
straight mark across contours
impossible to depict on the page:
an ancient rift zone where the river was
downfaulted a thousand feet: if this
isn't what makes me I don't know
what does: years: and what rises
as smoke over Kinne Brook, gray

against grayer day, under
the expanding cumulus cloud field,
an energetic disturbance
aloft: the company picked
over the last narrow stopes
in the emery mine
a century back, the visible supply
expended, the mill that ground a ton
an hour another asset
depreciated to worthlessness:
                                                            along
the ankle-deep river leaflace-winged
green darners hover
lower than bent maples
skimming rock-tumbled ripples:
                                                                no
matter what clarifies
my relief at proper names,
the inexpressiveness of the world
as I see it onscreen prevails, the plugin
operating in compatibility mode
force quits the winds' music
of there to here: the interior
temperature falls
to sixty amid emptiest
sunblown middleday:
                                            I learned
another detour through outlying
hills where Temik 15G
soaked rocky topsoil,
wrecked a rill,
ruined wells,
but the town extended

the water main:
                              a location
-based reminder:
                              in this light,
the whisky glows in its glass,
in the oversized ice
cube's tiny flaws
as it melts, but outside, from a plot
of muddy grass still almost green
on a fogged December
dusk, the lampshade is red,
the light through
kitchen curtains is red, and nothing
else is any color
but uneven: at the clinic,
I receive another six-month
reprieve from bloodletting:
the broken news searches
a phrase, seasonally
sectioned and lost
by an abandoned railtrack
rising above the riverside
where everything's overdue:
interrupted: where was I:
                                        the land
-marks are not incidental: the world
no longer extends as far
as memory's residue, but
below bluing skies the pond is still
low today between the milled
pavement of Center Street and the skylit
windshields on the turnpike beyond,
just .68 inches of rain this month:

the outbound mind:
I can't understand the full
implications of the uncertain
profit in these conversions,
the nights that morning doesn't
recognize, days off, days on
a hilltop trying to see past
the horizon, the windshadow,
the syntax of hi-vis ribbons tied to
twig tips in the woods, hot-pack tamped
to fill potholes, clarifying late-day
light, the unabolished self,
anything revelatory in its
diminishment:
                    black knot
galled the snowbowed plum
we didn't prune before
budbreak:
            we hacked it down,
burned the branches:
                              and just below
Tekoa, two lanes expand
to three for the climb: scrub
oak and pitch pine emboss
scratched strata of mica slate
over a brushfire scar: a rattlecan
sunset overloads a few pixels
but reveals the other
-wise unseeable patterns:
and contrails evaporate into
edgelessness, micronarratives
of exile:
            what day

doesn't feel composed
of obstructions: even the sun
gets filmed by cloud cover, like the subject
I elide and then restore
in a memo as if to clarify my
own weeklong absences
from the most familiar auto
-corrected history: but this new
crisis is built from the scraps
of the previous crises
and the unsettled index
of opinion:
                    everything
post-peak:
                    the woods' understory
and overstory, fuel for fire
weather: 89 octane, 42 cetane,
E 85, FlexFuel: scent of unburnt
hydrocarbons, sand spilled
by the pump to soak a diesel overflow,
sand spilled for traction
on the data-scraped slope,
Scarboro Brook's surge beside
delaminating pavement, a defeat
device for the emissions check,
a brute-force device to ease
the ascent:
                    one wing flaps up
in an asphalt-scouring wind
but the rest of the sparrow
is pulped in the lane, another
multipath ghost reflected between
a steel tower on Steerage Rock

and an unshielded RCA input
to a dusty screen someone still
watches: a coding break to consider
the decomposition of a freak
year, underwintered and annulled
by its own vanishing:
                                        but the afterlife
genuflects before preprogrammed
hillsides, small pond skinned with ice,
all that's unquantifiable:
                                              a simple circuit
from Hockanum's lowlit stubble
to Pollux for the commentaries
of windworn range and the scrutinies of shivering
oak leaves dwindled and dry but still
fastened to branches
after every other tree
has slipped its obligations: and then
home to patch up the sequence
that cannot withstand its own
strategies: whatever last refuges
from thinking too long or too little
about depletion or excess, like freezing
rain barely enough
to register on the pressure
-treated plank of a deck
attached to a house on an acre
of ex-farmland now frost-glazed
grass, or twenty million barrels
a day: not what was but what wasn't:
tick up the thermostat, tick it down:
the script could seem unique
but memory holds itself

together only through the fatigue
life of its alloys, the graceful
degradation even as discrete
components fail:
         this day's
like all the others,
downgraded to theory
before I even notice
it's gone: whatever
one can return to: nothing: blown
tire carcass, tailgating SUV: if you know
the current state, you can predict the future
state:
   fickle:
       and a late-night snow
overwhites morning's solid-state disk,
blanks three lanes of blacktop, collects
on the new gantries overhead,
roils by laser sensors that scan
laminated glass for transponder, flash
cameras that read a plate number,
record a face's nose-mouth angle
on a seven-year backup:
the stated purpose to save eight hundred
hours of vehicle delays a day
and up to seventy-eight hundred tons of greenhouse
emissions a year, but under
this revenue-neutral snow, this
nanotech snow, this Pantone-process
snow, all real movement ends
and the mythos of the material
world submits to the unofficial
accounts of an extant

melancholy: the name was changed
to avoid mistakes in delivery:
an unmarked cruiser,
the unremarked self:
the questionnaire requires only
ten minutes to complete, and your
responses are anonymized:

distance
makes the wires sag, but is this
a decision or an abdication
of a decision: one's voice
gets hoarse from explaining: a selloff
of all holdings: the industry's credit
and debt cycle affects the local
prices, so my appointment
with a hillside remains provisional,
but every time I walk the woods
with the dog I hear ravens calling
from derelict pines just below
the ridgeline: there's no
promise of exclusivity
on the back end, just tractor
tire tracks through an unconscious gray
field, regular morning passage past
that, a method of staying within
the economies of a twenty-first
-century truce with anecdote
and other unreconciled
losses: let the dead be
dead, unbroken by time's
recoveries:

a private ritual: garage
to sideroads to state route to divided

expressway to arterial surface
road to sideroads to parking lot: the left
turn here to avoid the light, the right
to be alone a little longer
each day with the comforts
of immoderation and climate
control and tempered glass
sidelites to block the geophony
until the gauge drops
almost to E:
                    but the human
mind is expert at filling vacancies,
inventing a few words to revamp
the voids in the sentence, wheeling
megawatts through a thousand-mile line
to balance demand across the grid,
buzzcutting some sumac groves
and digging foundations for six homes
to occupy the last lots on Bardwell Street:
next time I pass, two men apply
a black tar membrane to poured concrete
before the builder backfills with gravel,
then dirt: time after that, new
year, light spills through
argon-filled double-pane windows
in a two-by-six-framed wall clad
with extruded polyvinyl chloride
shaped into clapboards
impressed with a pattern
that simulates woodgrain,
and an Audi idles
in the driveway, wreathed
in water vapor, nitrogen

dioxide, benzene, soot, sulphur
dioxide, and a cold air mass
held in place by a high-pressure system
this subfreezing day: and I, even
idler in my own half-life, watching
where stunted pines once were: your cloud
storage is almost full: you have
358.3 MB remaining: please
upgrade your account to one
of the available plans: the curve
of apparently random events
can reset the process, but we
remain uncertain of what the process
encompasses: subsequent studies could not
duplicate the results, and tires tint
the snow the way everything sullies something
else: your life stains mine, mine
stains yours, and atmospheric aerosols
scatter light beamed from sinking sun
so it flares red, which also stains snow:
the hindsight bias of bare black branches
mutilating plain February ferric
sky and another pointless night
spent counting the all-time
views: an erased history:
recommended for you:
snow,
wind, night: so many
obliterations:
two
figures preserved after the briefest
warmth refreezes:
we might extend

the question of what forms
a complete thought in the direction
of morning's first eastern gestures, but
the screen's auto-dim setting returns
us to darkness and the sound
of traffic continues outside:
the problem of living in a polity
is that the wind still does make
your skin ache: I didn't point
out a single pothole and took
all the town lines, but understanding
always offers a reduction:
the evidence of authority
is everywhere in broken snowdrifts,
the clarity of satellite view
zoomed in so close the fenceposts leave shadows
on ground with an almost real texture,
or the refinements to the local
vernacular: the marked lane
violations, the market
indifference:
                    I spend evenings tracing
maps and days getting lost
among signless roads and
the limitless and illegible rhetoric
of infrastructure evolved
over centuries, but couldn't
say what meaning a gray-planked
barn in a field on Hyde Hill
articulates, or why
observation feels like
and unlike consumption,
but there has to be another method

of getting from here to
the unapproachable feelings:
the world is self-replicating, profuse,
abundant, even in afternoon light,
and a mile downhill, in a cutting
through steep banks, the microclimate drops
the air temperature ten
or fifteen degrees, and cryptographs
and miniglyphs in day-glo pink
paint mark where the road may be
safely dug:
                drive as if
                                your kids lived here:
I can't defer
to whatever knowledge of the past
has broken through the perimeter
of regrets a single week can fashion
from a loyalty oath to wind shear
or the transactions involved in trying to
forget one's character: the independent
study counted forty-eight hundred
vehicles per day, on average, using
this thirty-foot roadway, at least half
of them rattling the loose manhole
cover, and the system
of obligations burdening
a belief seems inevitable in
its context of 99¢ coffees, any size
styrofoam cup and snap
-on, no-spill plastic cap,
or a wait for someone
to switch on the machine
and reset the price to zero:

the rush to thread oneself back
into another delay because
we can't bear not to be
first: the battery has no memory
effect, but will last only two years
and cannot be replaced without damage
to the unit:

                    the rain-lit
afternoon asks the ontological
questions, and the decreasing radius
curve reveals the hill's function rather
than the road's, and the vertical
scenery addresses whatever
remains unspoken because I've lost
the breath and the will, but the billboard
looks at itself first to frame
time: and how is the world
restored to me from a remote server:
it's not:

            only one or two cloudshadows could
dim this valley, but don't, and the three
-to-four-hundred-year-old hemlocks
escape the preemptive cuts: the wood's
not worthless but not worth enough,
so as winters warm each
year the wooly adelgid
skeletonizes the trees:
claim it quick, all
the oscillations of a mellotronic
midday in goner hilltowns,
winddwindled houses crammed
on southface slope, CVV-coded
minimalisms of habit:

a sideyard's plastic pots of deadheaded
zinnias, four-chambered appraisal
tremored at 161 bpm, hubcap
lost in subshrub virescences,
thimbleberry bosk:
                                        powerless
to paraphrase tributary
from source to spillway, stream
to sound, all its panorhythmic
paragraphs: low articulations
along black-rock diabase,
arkosic sandstone banks,
clauses folded into currents:
so I search the underlying
network, the fading class IV
roads that backchannel me,
village to woodlot:
                                        sun
-screen my calls:
                                    I'm out:
leverage the lowest-keyed
loneliness, a barriered bridge
without decking, its pilings
sediment-scoured, the only
way across this gorge:
                                            it's not
an expression of acute crisis
or a bright-line rule:
not the most commented, most viewed:
the sacred questions remain
notional no matter how often
we recite them, but the past
can be accumulated, bundled,

sold off:

I don't need to graph
my decay:

like everyone else,
I seek only the least
inconvenience,
the least disruption, a day
defined less by what happens
than what doesn't: the impoverished
sunrise in an unrevoked sky
explains itself
historically via the eyes of those
squinting into it while a radio
voice enunciates the extent
of the burnt
neighborhoods elsewhere, the losses
computed in dollars: whatever
I came to know of legal
barriers to entry came
from passing through a town
where zoning bylaws specify
houses built on lots no smaller
than three acres:

the last rise
to the town hall gains a hundred
and fifty feet in less than half a mile,
but what good is a government
without at least the advantage
of seeing the entire horizon
smoothed into folklore: all the mechanisms
of simultaneity have acquired
privileged status, but you can still track
your package's cross-country

progress, or watch the descending
sun's broken rays among the boles and boughs
of trees you own in only one
sense, and the cloudcolors
quarried from your nostalgia cancel
all bonds: the audible
frequencies of birdsong, the utility
bills, the trips home, the last
error of a late-hour
broadcast, the production
freeze on grievance, the low-information
deer browsing the office park's dark
edges, the has-been, the never-was, all
the visual signifiers
of yearning:
                they arise naturally, seem
inevitable:
              the never
-to-be:
          and as you drive yourself
each day drives you farther
from anything that matters,
which isn't matter: the wrinkles in
this topography offer a poignant
index of cultural disarray: but
a folded, handwritten cue
sheet promises that the false
equivalency between a Wednesday
in early March and the contractual
imperative will not become a point
in the past to mourn: an autobiography
consisting primarily of a sawtooth
elevation profile and the ten

thousand or so shadows ungreened branches
make across my bare arms this
unseasonable season's day: a sideslope's
six scattered grazing horses still shaggy
against cold until winter's amnesty ends
in all the irreducible infinitives
and everyday failures that no new
architecture of logic can
mitigate:
            a rift in the cloud
pall allows the delinquent
sun to dramatize the glacier
-galled slopes of Tom and Nonotuck,
stippled maple tips and silvered pines
like a language without past
or future tenses, but where Alvord
curves a car's carved off
the bark from twin trees, and salt
stains the inability to manage
estrangements that turn toward
memorylessness: a mosaic
of fields and woodlots, a function,
a fiction: what the measurements
established: the hassle of gutter
glass, oversight of these laid-off
riverbends amid re-engineered
daylight and the privatization
of all movement:
                        blisters of days-old snow
gone granular along shadowed
blacktop edges, flecked with bark
and soot and sand and grit
to tally the ecologies

of unquestioned concession,
know-nothing nature shedding
selves to sustain the unarchived
diaries of days put to no use
except the registration
of predictability's
predicament, the way
the black twig apple blooms
too soon and the forecast rain arrives
as ice and breaks another
afternoon to its essentials: I wipe
the smudge a finger leaves on a scratched
lens, but lose an unemployable
focus on the narrow hollow
in Lyon Street where a branch fell
into the top smoking layer of bitumen,
a road roller compacted
it, and then a year's
weather wore it away to nothing
but the shape of its absence:
and these evaluations
of this plot and that one, nineteen acres
subdividable, perc test and market
comps, a run-on sentence running on
fumes:
            nothing erases boundaries
between the descriptive impulse
and the biotic equivalent of twenty
thousand miles of power
lines:
          still:
                  I will
weaponize forgetfulness

beyond all pursuits of profit
on someone else's ability
to profit on someone
else's ability to incur debt:
the immediate aftermath
of the slimmest margins counting
down the past beside a leaning
backyard fence through whose gaps
white-throated sparrows flicker
and churr suggests an orientation
toward outcomes, a decision
evaluated post hoc: the undergrowth's
immodesty screens its own tanglings,
the pitch of the sculpted yard limits
the gaze, the homes clad in fiber-cement
shingles contemplate bare beds of dyed mulch
girdling spindly saplings, but
the late-day sunlight overshares
its opinions and disregards
the responses as it too recedes
beyond Whippernon Hill: everything's
turning away the way it always
has: an addiction
to wishing, how cones cluster
near the top of a seventy-foot spruce
in this fumbled twilight, how a clock
stopped for years at eight-forty-four
expresses current habits more
than previous ones:
repeat the lie over and over, like
the stage 2 drought ending in endless
yellow pixels north of Clesson Brook:
expect disappointment until

radar reveals otherwise:
988 mb just offshore, weak
static stability, worsening
daytime conditions:
                                        water
weeps from a gutter
clogged with old maple keys:
                                                        days
darken and lighten like used-up
contrivances: days run through the same
interruption engine decomposing
the crucial pronoun
into minor echoes of ignored
testimonies: days operate
at a lower level of abstraction: days
import constituent traits:
days decimate days:
                                        this imbalance
in the square viewer remains
uncropped:
                        the future's fixed
already, and I don't want to admit
how much of my life went into
throwaway achievements:
                                                so I
quantified my complaints:
                                                a school
bus leads a line of cars along
a two-lane road's shredded
halogen dayglare, stopping
at this driveway, that one, the next:
a rules-based system: this
vehicle stops at all RR crossings:

at all our crossings: my
inconclusive mind's another
unlisted spec house, but the psychic
disorientation of sunset's
unwound phenomena plays across
the streaked windshield, its variations
invisible photographically, vanishing
at 1040 mph: a monopoly
on the exterior, the grid
underlaying the terrain invisible
until you zoom in on it: simple
electric pulse in the synapse,
Speedpass+ app with three ways to pay
and save, matrix of truant seasons, Markov
sequence to approximate a life,
this life:
                and yes you can notice
the absence of difference:
                                        it depends
on the quality of input,
but all the 2.5-micron
particles lodge in the lungs, infiltrate
the bloodstream like oxygen
does:
          steel-belted
beliefs sustain far more than
monumentary feelings, and the sky
selects a superfine mist
to translate the morning,
and drops nozzle down for hours:
someone else wrote the script
I follow, no matter how
much I disregard

the manufacturer's intentions
for the machine:
so the sno-mo
trail that borders the stereo
-phonic field traces a
doggereled windrow
and breaches an eighteenth-century
farmhouse's stone wall, lichen's
etched testament,
a stash of emptied
whisky nips by a firepit:
inexorable:
un-exitable:
in the woods, impossible
to tell what's a kinglet's chiptune
intro, what's a faulty seal: but
the received world underwrites
my discontent as if there were an obvious
use-value in an exurb indemnified against
whatever knowledge of past practices
can paywall a flooded valley: a watershed:
another VPN to spoof
a position:
a second
language of SAE
standards and torque specs,
the slough of a bouldered doubletrack
mudded by 4x4s and far
from the solace of usual
monotonies, all
the bad offers refused
for worse ones:
no matter

how often I've imagined
my experiences as arbitrary
and transient, no matter
the artificial scarcities I've
witnessed steering into another
roadblown sundown on
Old Turnpike while surveilled
by a state trooper, no matter the relics
of an eroded order in
a syndicated wind,
some trending altocumulus
fleece, and three dozen steel
pails tapping sugar maples,
or the immensities of long-chain
polymers tangled and bleaching
within a merge lane's banked
brambles, Ruggles Hill invests only
in its own vulnerability
study: the silver beeches are structured
only as trees: root, trunk,
limb, leaf: they exist
in time, change as I change:
a prepackaged strategy,
or what my own blinkered wreckage
resists: the natural forever, the vintage
blue of exterior decorating,
immemorial afternoons,
this shoulder season's love affair
with distance, the agency
of a four-hundred-mile wind
field scraping NNE along the coast:
I wanted to hyphen the tone:
even before it was gone:

but failed:
                    the invisible airborne
dust near the flashing red
at the bottom of the descent
is 92%
iron, plus steel
fibers and carbon motes flaked
off the semi-metallic brake
pads:
          a suitable concept
of efficient friction:
                                   another
blunt slant of being
salvaged from rugged uplands,
another I-am insistence
in the voice I use only
for talking to myself:
a murmur to perform the semantic
work of rendering identity
illegible:
                 a rusted satellite
tower at the decommissioned Nike
site between low-rise condo
complex and interstate
cloverleaf, and beyond a stand
of balsams, a föhn
flays the plate girders and beams
of an undone superstructure
that heckles the fundamental
frequency between earth and
ionosphere: 7.83 Hz:
as does an earth mover's
backup beeper:

we'll do whatever
we can to keep you
except keeping you:
but living's
its own habit,
and the experiential part
grinds up our denotative
world into contrived horizontalisms
of river, road, ridgeline, ruins
of a confidence in the compact,
remission of all obligations
and payments, incoherent
contingencies and storefronts
for rent here
at the ragged frontier
of the megalopolis:
the future
perfect of remorse, the permeable
membrane of my thinking
as exposed to a three-quarter
headwind's symphonic
barrage: and a car guns past
me, blows the stoplight:
a dual exhaustion: a delicate
border: a weather tax
on the unending,
the unendurable:
I have not forgotten
everything seen while solo
and, lacking the security
of language, now lost:
but that doesn't bring it back:
so I slip the sentence

around the absentee
form of another early morning's
drizzle manipulating
the currency of Fuller Brook as it
loops down through drumlins, the green
screen scape we tenant:
                                        this is
the best I can do:
                                   so I am
-ortize all my principles
over a twenty-year term,
and day cries uncle
as dusk effaces it,
and a buckthorn copse has already
foreclosed on the planned
obsolescence of the last
treed parcel on Rt. 47
until it too gets razed
for a 3000 sq. ft. 4 BR:
                                        I could
assume what evening winnows,
all the unsayable deletions,
but a retina can see a single
photon's flare at the threshold
of imagination:
                                 I can no longer
imagine the category
error of all the conversations
embedded in trees' metadata,
the frost-heaved stutter
bumps along Beldingville Road,
the nodded-off hubcap
propped against a mailbox post here

in the gray foothills of the break-
even point:
                    but redbuds thrive
in the halfshade of an ash grove
near Whately even after
daffodils have emerged
from a position of failure
to try to sustain the annals
of dispossession:
                              this is not
nothing, but nothing
ends: it only changes
forms:
          a generative grammar
that resists narrativity:
                                        as if
this mass riff on Mass., a joyride
from Bozrah to base, some
assisted daydreaming, a discourse
of cotton corespun tires with Kevlar
beads might all incentivize
the pluralities of solitude:
a rag of newsprint, a red
-winged blackbird clutching a reed:
a passive RFID tag
in the child's-size coil
mattress dumped in the drinking water
protection area: CSX boxcars
creak and knock between
exposed shale bluff and river,
and the wind's walk-on
role fast-forwards arpeggios
of dust from the Oxbow's

meadows:
the onscreen blip
just a fraud-detection script
in a runtime system:
I only
wanted some killer weather
to get outside in,
a souvenir of intimacy, some
summer morning petrichor, tire
hum on blacktop merging with
my accomplished inadvertence
while I cruise another week
never so surprising as when it
authenticates the comforts
of distress: but the oversize
load with two-trooper escort
and four-ways actuated
ascends the lee side of the worn
orogen in the climbing lane,
and at mile marker 31.6
the cloudbusted thesis
of this limited-access, tough-lack
monologue evicts all
the trauma I was quoted:
there's no
surplus remedy:
at the brackish
artificial pond edging the exit,
a yellow warbler's quiet
subsong salvages
an auto aesthetic, and I
wonder what winter
was for:

a casualty loss,
some shrapnel, lithic
remittances, the half-mile
path from sandpit to
FedEx depot, the landfill capped
last year the highest point in town,
the impermaculture of our
prosperities: Avery Brook
is just a fissure
embellishing a bluff face,
a deterioration of the first
person, an immigrant will
to filter all the wasted
energies of disinheritance:
none of this should surprise
me: the test pattern, the callback,
the deaccessioning,
the scheduled maintenance
of morning's melodic rain:
and if
rain audits all my ambitions,
if rain's modeshare explains
my habit of forgetting
everything I've forgotten,
the slowest hashing function
cannot trace the edges
of immunity or promise
self-determination:
it's just another mechanism
for sifting abundance: I
never wanted more than
to pass through here
unbothered, to escape

genealogy's abductions
because history hasn't
manufactured this blurred daylight,
or negated its sorrows:
the hand moves from steering
wheel to white page,
the eye scans the meadow's
spreadsheet, the rearview,
the blocked callers list,
the cross-device retargeting,
all the years that go
into an hourly wage:
                                        the problem
of last-mile delivery:
                                        at a certain
point, everything's a donation:
a detonation
of facts
and fates:
                    a halo
of modernization surrounds
this sovereign skyline, some
oversimplified hostility
between April's outbreak
of blue squills and the embroideries
briars stitch along the riverbank,
or twists of tangled treetrunks
the microburst left in the background:
the radar signature showed the high
probability of spinups:
but the absence of usefulness
is not purpose:
                              I scrolled back

through proliferations:
hill blocks view:
sunflowers can't miss:
a plastic six-pack
yoke, an eternal
current, an annual
report: I expected to feel
splintered: but the issue is
structural: spatial: and the present
mislays verisimilitude:
Fomer Road has been regraded,
and Damon Pond's spill through a sluice
is purely transactional: the no
trespassing sound of closure
decays in the reverberant
space of a white pine grove,
another minor wind-whine:
and then evening dislodges
all the aimless repetitions blown
on long-haul transport
for the sake of itemizing
my moods: an unencounter
with day's frayed outskirts,
an annulment of autonomies,
and the most private spaces fall
beyond acceptable values and go
into limp mode:
                                        tires mumble
on and on and on on
pavement ribboned with crack
sealant, but usually speech
isn't expressed as a ratio: we
all need to address our

deficiencies: it's only
business, like a V formation
of Canada geese, each one winging
in the upwash of the bird
ahead:
                an over-the-horizon
array fires
a missive,
demolishes the costs
of compliance: the same old
engine that makes everything
possible:
                have you seen
my disfigured mountain,
have you seen my flyaway
empire:
                the voice
-activated system reroutes me,
afternoon races toward its
routine singularity,
the monthly mileage total
resumes, the industry's new
profile bleeds expectations,
the visible geoengineering
expires in a desire
line crossing the grass
at a diagonal and vanishing
past the single maple left
standing on the hilltop, the verbal
errancies coexist with
a twenty-minute downpour
that yields to isotropic
skybreaks and the remnants

of an internally combusted I,
in between, unreachable,
elsewhere, otherwise—

ACKNOWLEDGMENTS

Some of these poems were originally published in *Bennington Review*, *Bomb*, *The February Project*, *ONandOnScreen*, *Oversound*, *Poetry Northwest*, and *Tampa Review*. Thanks to their editors: Samuel Amadon, Geoff Bouvier, Lucy Clark, Liz Countryman, Tom Devaney, Michael Dumanis, Erin Malone, and Petro Moysaenko.

Portions of "Cascading Failures" were published in the chapbook *Cascading Failures* (Greying Ghost). Thanks to Carl Annarummo.

Thanks also to Paige Ackerson-Kiely, Geoff Bouvier, Sarah Goldstein, Claire Hero, and Andrew Zawacki for reading versions of this manuscript and offering valuable advice.

The phrase "at the threshold / of imagination" is taken from "The human eye can detect a single photon, study finds," by Deborah Netburn, *The Los Angeles Times*, July 19, 2016.

Joshua Harmon is also the author of the poetry collections *Le Spleen de Poughkeepsie* (winner of the 2010 Akron Poetry Prize) and *Scape,* as well as the essay collection/memoir *The Annotated Mixtape,* the novel *Quinnehtukqut,* and the short fiction collection *History of Cold Seasons.* He lives in western Massachusetts.

Printed in the United States
By Bookmasters